# Breakout

Other books of poetry by Victor V. Valenote (published under pseudonym, Thomas Walker):

Ashes In My Skull

Book III......Conundrum En Passant

Incendiary Forefronts and Other Commotions

# Breakout

poems by

Victor V. Valenote

**Thomas Walker Publications**
Eagle River, Alaska

For Information:

Thomas Walker Publications
26010 White Spruce Drive
Eagle River, Alaska 99577
Ph: 907-306-2012
Email: victorv@bdsak.com

Library of Congress Control Number: 2016908900
ISBN 978-0692724958
First Edition

1  3  5  7  9  10  8  6  4  2

To
Thomas Walker.

*Late at night when the moon is high,*
*the coyote talks to me.*
*"Don't forget the Learn'd Astronomer......*
*don't forget the Halls of Misanthropy."*

# Contents

Angel's Trumpet ........................................................................1

The Ode to Endless Love .......................................................2

The Ghost Parade........................................................................4

The Mourning Sun ...................................................................5

Across the Universe / 4th Time Around....................................6

Recognition of Their Sigh .......................................................7

Stones of My Mind ..................................................................8

In Life's Last Scene (a song for whomever) ...........................10

A Song for Virginia ................................................................12

Would You Believe......? .........................................................14

The Blues: a contradiction between getting IN and getting OUT....15

The Eighth Mask ....................................................................16

In Memory of Maggie B. ........................................................17

Nothing....................................................................................18

Yuma .......................................................................................19

No Direction Home..................................................................20

Would You Like Some More Coffee (notes from a 9:00 a.m.

meeting)...................................................................................21

Right Behind............................................................................22

Still Standing............................................................................23

Spot Light ......................................................................................24

Repetitious Need ...........................................................................25

The Hunger ...................................................................................26

Legend of Timothy Shay (8th grade poetry submission)....................27

The Thing is You.............................................................................30

Hey Angel, Angel............................................................................31

December 21, 2045 .........................................................................32

One Big Ceremony..........................................................................37

When I'm Alone..............................................................................38

One Step Beyond............................................................................39

Kaleidoscope Eyes ..........................................................................40

Laughing at Your Denial..................................................................42

The Last Ride .................................................................................43

If Only Just Good-bye.....................................................................44

The Ghost of a Lost Love's Soul c. 1740, London, coming to greet

an unknown suicide victim...............................................................45

Beyond Survival (not another waterfall) ...........................................46

To the Wolves.................................................................................48

Throw Caution to the Wind ............................................................50

April May ......................................................................................51

Mutiny on Floor Twenty-Nine.........................................................52

Plastic Songs in the Broken Ceremony .............................................53

Where are you, Sister Blue ...............................................................54

Forgetfulness ..................................................................................55

Red, Red, Dawn..............................................................................56

Wobble-wobble-wobble......Flip ......................................................57

The Erotic Nightmare...........................................................................58

The Small of Your Back ....................................................................61

Imagine a Dream (a song for April) .................................................62

Burying Alive.....................................................................................63

The Gambler ......................................................................................64

Spellbound ........................................................................................66

The Undefeated One .........................................................................67

Summer Fling.....................................................................................68

Office Life...........................................................................................69

The Oak Tree .....................................................................................70

A Good Morning from Hell ..............................................................71

The Celibate Man ..............................................................................72

Lost Memory Gained.........................................................................73

Inside .................................................................................................74

Royal Companion ..............................................................................75

Before You're Old..............................................................................76

On and On it Goes ............................................................................78

The Monkey-Faced Spider ................................................................79

Hippopotomonstrosesquipedaliophobia ..........................................80

Another Wad of Paper........................................................................82

On the Sea Floor ...............................................................................83

Never Before the Sacrifice ................................................................84

Exhale ................................................................................................85

The Land of Dick and Jane...............................................................86

Sail on, Silver Smile ..........................................................................87

On My Way Home .............................................................................88

Taking Precedence................................................................89

Halfway to My Sundown......................................................90

Perhaps You .......................................................................91

The First Five Seconds ........................................................92

A Ten-Minute Poem ...........................................................93

I Wonder If God Has a Patent...............................................94

Another stupid fucking poem that starts with 'and'.................95

Misanthropic Optics............................................................96

Uncovering the Future..........................................................98

Self-Recognition.................................................................99

So Many Things ................................................................100

Get Up and Go..................................................................101

The Last Prayer.................................................................102

# Breakout

# Angel's Trumpet

I hear......the swish of a blade slicing through empty air;
I feel cold and passionless.
I need a woman, a beautiful young woman
to cure me of my wickedness
as I lie in the fields of a deadly sanity,
all wrapped up in blankets woven with misery.

I hear......the watch exploding with every second,
its hands signal half-remembered images.
A scarecrow cries to me, he really is scared
that he's being compared......to nothing.
I said, you shouldn't play with fire,
and put my cigarette out in his face.

I hear......the flame blazing higher and higher.
It's all just smoke in the heart
as each phantom breeze makes you wander
into the depths of your own faith.
For 'tis nature which provides us
with flowers and beasts.

I hear......bones crushing as the clouds shift in the sky
like plasma, a whole neighborhood
of blood and empty dreams.
Mistaken fantasies give way to new doubts,
and I doubt that there is
a beautiful young woman in my future.

Victor V. Valenote

# The Ode to Endless Love

Look at me going down hell's road,
trying to find my humble abode,
and now it's time to sing the ode......to endless love.
The Church of Seduction is in neon,
the glamour girls are sniffing Freon,
the way they look at you they must be on......some godlike love.

Red, red rooms and a crystal ball,
naked eyes down every hall;
don't close a door if you're afraid to fall......deep in love.
Come with me my insanity, my misery;
come with me, let's fall......deep in love.

Long black hair and a silken dress,
what did you do to get in this mess?
Don't turn around unless, unless......you want my love.
Come with me my insanity, my misery;
come with me, let's undress......you want my love.

The signals are green but I have to stop,
the lynx run and the rabbits hop,
lay your head back, it's time to drop......this liquid love.
Come with me my insanity, my misery;
come with me, and you will get......this liquid love.

The lights are getting stronger,
the ceiling looks longer,
and now it is time to conquer......your true, true love.
Look at me going down hell's road,
trying to find my humble abode,
and now it's time to sing the ode......to endless love.

My love inside is oozing.
My soul outside is cruising;
cruising down a road to Hell,
but Hell......Hell is my paradise!

If you've ever been to heaven
then I tell you......it sure feels nice!

What's good is bad, what's bad is good,
and that's all right with me.
Love feels so nice
but like a temple made of ice
it melts down eventually.
Time is essential, think of its potential,
and act accordingly.
Knowing, growing, wild winds are blowing
across a cold and frozen sea.

I need some tongue, along my lung,
you know where it is that I breathe;
and feeling no apprehension
I stand at attention,
to kiss your eager face.
A touch of silk, a touch of lace,
a frozen heart tries to embrace;
with legs wrapped around ever so tight,
milking my dreams throughout the night,
and filling the needs of Satan's delight.

# The Ghost Parade

Wake up at dawn and ask for wine.
Off in the distance you will see a sign
with letters on fire, burning and bright;
letters so tall they drift out of sight.
Then suddenly, they will begin to recede,
and squinting your eyes you can slowly read.

Stand on the bed, touch the sky;
follow the whale, you will know why.

So, she stood on the bed, reaching way up high;
she touched the ceiling and didn't ask why.
To her amazement it turned to a watery steel;
her hand slipping through with a mercury-like feel.

A killer whale of silvery hue;
follow the sun, he says to you.
Come swim with me and the golden fish;
just close your eyes and make a wish.
We'll chase it forever the world around;
we'll look everywhere until it is found.

And with each crystal raindrop upon your head
another useless memory is shed.
The silver whale just keeps on swimming,
with polar bears dancing and grinning.
The ice-capade, the ghost parade;
the soft immaculate snowy breeze
whisking through your thoughts like floating trees.
Spinning madly in the bright winter haze
obscuring all life into a stone-like daze.

So, keep up with the whale, never let it out of your sight
and you will never have to see, the darkness of night.

# The Mourning Sun

Don't ever let anybody put you down,
don't ever let anybody say
that they're better......better than you,
don't follow their way.
Because you're better than everyone
when you've seen the mourning sun
yes, you are better than everyone
when you've got a loaded gun
Point it toward your heart,
are you afraid to take the chance?
just as you are afraid of joy;
and afraid of romance.
but you don't have to tell me
because it is already showing
how you'll never make it anywhere
because you're so afraid of knowing
what it is like to be in real love
what it is like to lose control
what it is like to open up your eyes
what it is like to give your soul
you see, I feel like a bird;
a bird that cannot fly.
for when your life is missing love
you just want......want to die.
but the freedom in your smile
can rid of all the pain
that creeps into my mind
like the pour......pouring rain.
Through the windows of reality,
through the doors of broken dreams
through everything that matters
oh, so it seems......oh, so it seems.

# Across the Universe / 4th Time Around

Celebrate......

the birth of BEAUTY and the birth of RAIN,
the birth of LOVE and the birth of PAIN,
the birth of ART and the birth of HEATHER;
for all these things they go together......

like spring,
like flower
and the mysterious power;
of rose and thorn
and the hearts they've torn.

like passion
like fury
and the destined worry;
of lion and cage
and the poet in rage.

like fool,
like romance,
and the fortuitous chance;
of light and thunder
and the spell they're under.

like lace,
like leather,
and the stormy weather;
for all these things
they go together......

like the brightest star and the sky,
like the whitest bird and the feather
fly-flying high and fly-flying forever;
all for 'the birth' and all for HEATHER.

# Recognition of Their Sigh

They were standing in the corner of the station
in need of designation in the rain.
Waiting and waiting, waiting and waiting,
and without a destination came the train
to take them away to some other town;
quite simply put, to remove their frown.
So, they climbed aboard the empty ocean train
and said good bye to all of their pain.

No one knows where they are going
but their destiny is clearly showing,
glowing in the jewel of their smiles.
And no one ever seems to figure out
that love is life and is all about
the recognition of their sigh.

Two smile, two sigh, and neither ask why
they hear the sounds of sunshine
creeping through the window near.
They hear the doldrums' divinity
pounding in a soft rhythm of heartbeats.

They feel the waves and the ocean
'twas Neptune's devotion;
soothing in the naked summer sun.
Eyes to eyes and two more sighs.
Hips to hips and then their lips

```
e    l  o  i        l
  xp   d  n      i  k  e
              g              a
co       en       j
   s  o  g  i       e  w  l
     m        c              e  .
```

Victor V. Valenote

# Stones of My Mind

Down around the alleyways......the back roads
        of my mind,
a road is paved with many stones;
a mason that is TIME.
one stone tells a story of memories cas

                              c a
                              d
                                 ing

down a city sewer, through an iron grating
to a far and distant world,
        its sky illuminating
with silver seas and golden trees,
        where a checkered dog is waiting.
"Welcome all......fool or foe, come help me
find my bone.
It is not here, it is not there, we'll have to
        check another stone.

This one here has a message, every word embossed,
"a well-wisher's dream, another stone is tossed"
back there over your shoulder before the curse
        is lost......I'd like to let you out of here
        but you've been double crossed.
Yet have no fear, the rats are here, you'll
never be alone; just keep on contemplating,
never hesitating......to turn another stone.

Some stones are for tomorrow,
some stones are for the past
as rats scurry in the gutter
through empty bottles where broken glass
        shines a mysterious glow of moonlight
upon a very special stone, a stone to surmise.
"The poet learns more from fools
than fools learn from the wise."
Now these are just a few and if you'd like

Breakout

to see the rest
you'll have to join me on the journey,
        join me on the quest.
But the road is very, very long
        and there are many stones to find
down around the alleyways......the back roads
        of my mind.

Victor V. Valenote

# In Life's Last Scene (a song for whomever)

As my youth faces the firing squad, I have one last request:
Let me be in love......real love!
For then would it be an easeful death;
but real are the dreams that leave me with lustrous eyes
full of sorrow, full of tomorrow.
Tomorrow is time, time is nature,
and 'tis nature that tosses me about
like a carcass in the mouth of a hungry lion.
And 'tis nature that makes my human heart
pound in rhythmic pain.
But calm is my smile, the devil's mask,
like a lily with its streaks of beauty;
on the outside......is divinity,
on the inside......a pounding of rhythmic pain.
I try to get angry, 'tis such a fast emotion,
always to be overcome by sorrow
like the tortoise and the hare.
Oh, if I were young again, if I were wise,
would a fire burn for me with magic in my eyes;
as half my failures go up in a cloud of smoke.

The happiest bond of love is the mystery of fate,
but there's so much hurt in the wait.
How long must I wait......how long must I wait;
for that final shot of redemption?
Like a flower in the forest, I long for the sun's rays
to shine down upon my withered, beaten soul.
For now, my voice comes across silent......horribly silent.

I oftentimes feel that I've never been born
and only when I meet a beautiful young woman named (        ),
will I live......the valiant glory of real love.
For all that I've ever been doing is waiting......for her!

Then, in life's last scene, we will walk along alone......
for alone we will walk for love

as together we will be in love
and together we will walk alone......
living and breathing as one;
one ceremony of open wounds
from the misfortunes of heartache,
from busted, broken, dreamy sensations;
but linger we will because we desire......
desire a similar pain,
desire a mutual existence
that is our freedom,
that is our destiny,
that is our reason for being;
being in love,
being together.

# A Song for Virginia

Throw stones
into the mouth of July,
I always asked why
and then she was dead;
Take a good glimpse,
a good look,
and his head shook,
filled up with lead.

She gallantly took
another step forward,
and headed toward
the starry, starry night;
finding him lying
in the very same place,
she covered her face
with hands of fright.

Fare thee well Virginia,
fair thee well,
only you could hear the bell
and it was ringing for me;
and when the water
begins to overflow,
I know that you'll know
what I need to be free.

------------------------------

She came to his company, she came to his side;
and with all his pain, she never denied;
the lonely broken feelings, the emptiness inside.

If she had one wish, she would take it all away;
the exorcism of misery, a demon goes astray;
and into her soul, his black thoughts for each day.

# Breakout

It's so hard to make the story come together with great sense;
for his world is getting larger, so complex, and so immense;
but she knows what it means, her time, now getting dense.

Yes, she knows what it feels like to be trampled upon;
the eyes in your head crack open, like a red sun at dawn;
and just like life, it is here and then it is gone.

Oh, the mind how it wanders, the mind how it squirms;
she comes to make peace, she comes to make terms;
and just like life, it is a book full of worms.

Victor V. Valenote

# Would You Believe......?

It happened one early morning
   as I awoke;

I heard the delicate footsteps
   of beauty;
and looking out of my bedroom window......

gallantly passing before my eyes,
a lady dressed in black......

the loveliest lady of all.

I thought to myself
how easy it would be to fall......
for her;

for beauty has left me
wondering......

wondering if she needs love,
wondering if she needs romance,
wondering if she needs a friend,
wondering if she'd give me the chance.

# The Blues: a contradiction between getting IN and getting OUT

I've hung my head low and
    cried in the rain;
I've lifted my head high and
    laughed at the rain;
and I tell you, each of those times
    I felt quite the same;

    like a fool......
    like a fool......
    like a fool......

yes, like a fool;
like a fool......with nowhere to go.

I've been in the jungle and
    to the top of the mountain;
I've been through the desert and
    across the great plain;
and I tell you, each of those times
    I felt quite the same;

    like a fool......
    like a fool......
    like a fool......

yes, like a fool;
like a fool......with nowhere to go.

# The Eighth Mask

The eighth mask is the best
for it is the mask of rest......

1. birth
2. wealth*
3. power*
4. fame*
5. love*
6. honor*
7. pain
8. death

Birth, hearth, here on earth
strive to stay alive

Those who cannot wear
any of the magic five
will always wear the mask of pain
until the eighth does arrive.

# In Memory of Maggie B.

Inside the graveyard
of busted, broken
dreams and hopes;
of lustful girls
in chains and ropes.

I always know when I am near it;
the curls, the scent, the gentle spirit.
And lying before me upon the ground,
to the earth she was abound.
Her arms and legs spread apart
exposing all except her heart.
Moaning and thrashing all about,
I decided to see what it was all about;
and seeping in, her eyes enflame
I know it will never be the same.

Soft and sleek aquatic motions,
crystal pearl of lakes and oceans,
and looking forward
the tombstone read,
"This one is for you,
her name is Dead."

# Nothing

Every time I see
a wide
and
open door
it reminds me
of how life should
be,
but the truth beholds;
life
is full of heartache.

Nothing is ever free.

So, you struggle
all of your life
to be free......
to prove that you
are more than
nothing,
but nothing,
is ever-free.

# Yuma

Hell is my paradise,
hell is my paradise.
If you've never been to heaven
then I tell you, it sure feels nice.

Every time I turn away,
I see the stars fading;
cascading,
cascading tears
over the fears I have
of losing you.

Every time I close my eyes,
your golden hair
blowing free,
touching me.
The gentle breeze
burns my heart;
a part of me is dying.

Victor V. Valenote

# No Direction Home

When she cried,
she imagined that I was hurting.
Yet hurting is a pain
that is weak and fragile,
a pain that I have defeated
again, and again.

But this broken promise
is true assassination
and has left her unfocused,
in a whirl of emotional turmoil.
She doesn't know which path to choose
because there isn't one available.

# Would You Like Some More Coffee (notes from a 9:00 a.m. meeting)

The establishment has been derived from the common mind.
I cannot liquefy a thought, but I see an inspiration before me.

I.      A lady in red is quality.

        Typical conversation bores me.
        I cannot concern myself with anything
        but beauty;
        (delicate beauty) --- with a rock the size of Pluto!

II.     I cannot focus any(more).

        A thought comes in and it fluctuates
        with the burning intensity of a peyote trance.
        That which appears unimportant to the
        mortal eye often receives a value
        like an olive tree to Vincent;

        (the lady is always there) --- to taunt / haunt me!

III.    Quality is a creative logic.

        For a man with half a brain,
        it always seems to work out this way.
        If there were a God;
        a God that created a Universe,
        not a light bulb, not a printing press,
        not a motion picture, but a Universe,
        why would he allow there to be pain?
        If he exists then he, does so in disgrace;

        (a lady cannot be god) --- that is the reversal of logic!

IV.     Sanctuary is in the lips.

        The root cause of desire is
        the harmonic nature of      beauty.

21

Victor V. Valenote

# Right Behind

I took her home,
I loved her three times,
and she wanted more.

That is why I like her;
like her lying there,
on the floor.
Her eyes staring
into mine
with hell lurking
right behind,
behind the door.

# Still Standing

In the shadow of your eyelids,
and the movement of a cheek.
You tear apart the strong,
and you nullify the weak.
Like a lioness on the hunt,
I'm the one that you seek.

But never have you come across
a soul as hard as me.
Petrified and frivolous,
ominous and carefree.
You take an axe to my side
as though I were a tree.

# Spot Light

Hindsight......
Cursed are the memories
that keep me tossing
and turning
through the depths
of a fathomless night.
Spot light......
cursed is the butterfly,
black with ruby eyes,
that is always in flight
somewhere in my mind.

# Repetitious Need

There is a demon
called solitude,
the side of loneliness
that is not so brightly lit.
The story is quite clear,
another day / another year
without proclivity.

For nothing but nothing
can replace
man's repetitious need
for physical female
companionship.

# The Hunger

I once tried to grasp a troubled heart
and in doing so......failed;
'tis the same illusion
of a certain summer day
when it was my kindness
that pulled the trigger,
that stopped the bird from singing.
Sometimes we do a wild thing,
as with one passion inside of another.
Now my spirit lies......withdrawn
unto itself; I who have been self-deceived,
I who have breathed love......as few ever do.
But often, the taste of honey
does not quench the appetite
of a hunting man......tortured;
hungered for so long,
and of course......the hungry will hunt
with reckless abandon.
What else could be expected?
My innermost soul has become shadowed
with the turning away.
It ceases to exist, and I wonder
why things couldn't work out
my way......just once;
at a time in my life when I needed
satisfaction like never before.
A chance for a needed inspiration,
a chance for beauty,
a chance for everything, everywhere;
humanity's unending struggle.

# Legend of Timothy Shay (8th grade poetry submission)

I wonder if Van Gogh perceived the world
the way that he painted it.
After all, painting is a coming together of the way we see;
poetry of the way we think (collectively)
......now there is a particular way
that I want to say a few words.

A......is for my girl
B......is for love
C......is for loneliness
D......is for pain
E......is for everyone and
F......is for the same
G......is for the butterfly
H......is for you
I......is for desperation and
J......a sky of blue
K......is for memories
L......we all know
M......is for togetherness
N......is time to let go
O......is for understanding
P......is the fate of man
Q......is for wondering and
R......is because he can
S......is for killing pain
T......is conqueror of all
U......is for so very few and
V......is for the greatest fall
W......is for ceremony
X......is for the season
Y......is all I ever hear and
Z......is for the reason

If you ever wondered why I stopped sending you my poems
it is because I know that you don't really care (give a fuck).
You can't, you just don't have the time.

......and I understand time.

It takes time to think;
it takes time to give a fuck.
A nanosecond is a lifetime for a minute.

......and I understand life.

We are supposed to have evolved from hunter/gatherer apes
into civilized human beings but we are still just slaves;
laborers of the mind working in the factory.
Your mind is bought and sold with food and shelter,
and you must not think on the factory's time......only yours.

......and I understand death.

The seedling of all fears;
the eternity of optimism;
the only truth that you can count on,
maybe.

......and I understand love.

Do you wonder if I really think the way that I write?
I have been thinking about memories, voluntary and involuntary
I have noticed that I sometimes think of you and don't know why
it is involuntary......the sound of a wave, the smell of perfume
I don't know what it is, one moment nothing, another and
I think of you [I am just using you because I am writ(h)ing to you]
not some dime store romance novel / network television story
(Oh Juliet come forth and see my love rise, ne'er to fall
I shall chasten thee with my sword......and I shall
kill all those who cause you pain......and I shall
stand by you until I die, to protect your sacred dreams
and all for the sake of your sweet kiss, your sweet love.)

## Breakout

((oh, sorry that I got a little carried away, I should've just said
that I cherished the times I spent with you.
an iceberg in my brain, a good one))
you never really can go too far as you've sees;
the snake is full of poison,
a good one, and you know what I mean.
I love my 8$^{th}$ grade language arts teacher, Ms. Fullalove.

......and I understand hate.

The foundation of all unhappiness.
Consumed by the miserable and their
involuntary reaction to displeasure.
Innate as human hunger,
and most likely responsible for our evolution.

I hate this poem.

Victor V. Valenote

# The Thing is You

Life is a comedy as well as a tragedy.
No one, alone, understands the ups and downs.
Shakespeare, he only understood the interpretation
of a time and a culture, a place and a society.

To those that climb the highest mountain,
to those that think they are at the top,
to those who sink to the depths of despair,
to those who think that they are not,

in life there are both known and unknown things
that are either living or dead......
physical (tangible, able to grasp with the senses
and with ease what is known as reality
for each individual......alone),
or emotional (little ticks in the mind
that make up a response to any or no stimulus);
it may be a thought containing a fish, a gun,
an angel, and a poet.

And of all the known and unknown things,
do you know the one thing that I hate the most?

# Hey Angel, Angel

Hey angel, angel in a paradise suit
hey angel, angel right out of the chute
you go falling, you go falling from me
hey angel, angel right out of the past
hey angel, angel never going to last
through the calling the calling of me
hey angel, angel the water feels fine
hey angel, angel won't you give me a sign
that you're falling, you're falling for me
hey angel, angel I love you so much
hey angel, angel, I am losing my touch
with real, reality.
hey angel, angel born to sweet delight
hey angel, angel I can't sleep at night
are you falling, are you falling for me?
hey angel, angel I howl at the moon
hey angel, angel please come home soon
I'm calling, I'm calling for you.
I've been through nearly half of a life
and I've never seen such a sharpened knife
I'm calling, I'm calling for you
Run through the meadows, fly through the trees
whatever you do, do what you please
I'm calling, I'm calling for you
It is nature I'm feeling, it is nature up close
such a strong and potent, lethal dose
now you're falling, you're falling for me.
You can curse the walls around and curse my name
you can take me for granted, take me for shame
I'm still falling, falling for you.
I'll run naked across the desert, or the arctic snow
I'll do anything, anything just to show
that I'm falling, falling for you.
hey angel, angel, a passionate treat
hey angel, angel make life complete
say you're falling, falling for me.

31

# December 21, 2045

Ecstasy in vision
is almost commonplace
hence the agony of frightful temptations
and telepathic insights of self-slaughter
resulting wounds from toxic substances
find a way into the bloodstream
cause hallucinations
schizophrenia, survival
a god refusing the fear of hell
beat yourself into intoxication
and cultivate insomnia
solemn ceremonies and assorted jewels
practical parabolic reflectors
inventions so profound (40 years later)
impossible to evoke
the bounds of chaos in an island universe
the magic of remoteness hangs in your eyes
in spite of everything
you cry for human imperialism
an absolute manifest
identical with being

my eyes are so dry, missing emotions

I lay my head down
record the rest
close to unconsciousness
beautiful woman I'd like to caress
looking so fragile in a long white dress
how do......you measure success?

I am an erotic heretic
but delusion does have its rewards
hordes and hordes of loneliness
did you ever feel so lonely that
you thought you were the only person in the world,

Breakout

and everybody else was dead
did you ever cut yourself
and laugh at the dripping blood
did you ever fire a gun into the heavens
hoping to kill god
Yet, when you drift off into sleep
everything is so peaceful, so perfect

you don't want me hangin' around
take me to the devil's lake
and leave me to drown
there is no doubt about it
love cannot be found
when you are not around
to say......how are you doin' today,
how are you doing?
you said there was no time to be my wife
but how'd you find the time to wreck my life

There was no sun, there was no king
the only thing left......my heartache to sing
my heartache to sing, my heartache to sing

seen too many pictures of a promise in disdain
you can burn every last one, babe
but the thought still remains

you can roll the past and smoke it away
I tell you babe, please don't stay......
without me, babe
please don't stay without me

hey, does it have you hypnotized
or is the melancholy madness disguised
around you, babe, all around you

five to twelve and no one's here
I think I'll go have another beer
without you, babe, without you

and to all the good people with happy news
I'm getting to fucked up to sing the blues
about you, babe, about you

running around, head to the ground
yeah, I can't wait
like a blackbird in a nest
I can't wait to be laid to rest
'twas you I loved the best

I've seen to many dreams dissipate
I buried myself in a mountain of hate
look around you
I'm there, I'm everywhere
so, when I come around the final bend
you had better be there
I'm talking about the end.

I'm gonna close my eyes
and count from one to ten
and you had better be ready to start again
or I'm going on without you, babe
going on without you

you never know what tomorrow will bring
another lovely song to sing
I don't feel like you need me anymore
all my energies are growing, babe
showing tears of anguish,
years of anguish

back to surreality,
surreality......that's me
hunted down like the wildebeest
roast me up for the feast around you

you don't believe in me, I don't mind
I don't mind the criticism everyone's looking for

mysticism of angels, angels
you know what I am thinking about, babe

if I didn't have to give up my penny dreams
tell all the people an end to the means
about you, yeah, about you
if you want to be in the great chariot race
you better run your horses some other place
a forgotten place
I told you, yes, look around you

I'd like to say I'm somebody
but what would you really call me
what would you call me?
nothing, absolutely nothing
not even a poet, babe, nothing

another pilgrimage to the place I was born
you know I think I'm torn
between the innocent and free
is there anyone who can see like me
come and see me, babe,
come and see me

the country is vast, wild and strong
Gulliver imprisoned but not very long
all around you, I warned you
all around you

if I came and dragged you out of your bed
would you go and tell everybody what I said
about you, yeah about you

I came from a mirror that you hold within
spinning back to the refrain
spinning back to the refrain
back to the pain
all around you

it's hard to sleep at the moment of your death
you know everyone could be the last breath
'tis a beautiful existence though
to know that life is limited
you can only go so far
before you collapse, perhaps
perhaps the ant feels the same
running around,
running around following the queen
I think I'll wind up somewhere
between here and outrage

every word ends a page
in a novel called 'sanctuary'
perhaps the little deer quietly
drinking water feels the same
waiting for the lion's claw
to begin the slaughter

and every now and then
I lift my head again
like a horse with a broken leg
won't you please put me down
I'm battered and beaten
I'm torn and defeated
how much longer must I beg
you to please put me down
won't you please put me down.

# One Big Ceremony

We walk along, alone......
for alone we walk for love;
as together we are in love
and together we walk alone......
living, breathing as one.

One big ceremony of open wounds
from the misfortunes of heartache;
from busted, broken, dreamy sensations.
But linger we do, because we desire;
desire a similar pain.

A mutual existence
that is our freedom,
that is our destiny,
that is our reason for being......
being in love, being together.

Victor V. Valenote

# When I'm Alone

I hear a voice from the cypress tree
saying you'll always be there for me.
I'll always believe the story it tells
of silver, of white, of chiming bells.

I think of your body next to mine.
I feel your love all the time
as I lay in bed and stare into space,
thinking of you and the smile on your face.

But the light in the window will always remind,
what it is like to be left behind.
Laughing footsteps from across the room
you sit by my side, it is never too soon.

I'll never give up, I'll never let go
of the passion we had, so let the blood flow
onto the floor in a deep scarlet hue
that makes me feel happy, makes me feel blue.

# One Step Beyond

I think that you are mine
I think that all the time
but I know that you are golden
and I know that I......am an ice machine
I'm so cold, I'm so cold
let your blanket cover me
come closer to me
with your blanket of misery
come closer to me

I think that black is white
I think that day is night
but I know that you are unkind
and I know that I......am in love again
I've been here before, I've been here before
a box of pain on the floor
come closer to me
a box of pain at your door
come closer to me

I think that in is out
I think that thought is doubt
but I know that you're in shock
and I know that I......am one step beyond
now you have a heart, now you have a heart
see what you can do
come closer to me
see if love is true
come closer to me.

# Kaleidoscope Eyes

I wish I could find a bit of paradise
I wish I could spend a moment alone with you
I wish I could share a delicate dream
with the lovely Kristen Blue
I wonder if she feels the rhythm of destiny
a facade I can see right through
from the moment I first laid eyes
on the lovely Kristen Blue
I don't really know what I was doing there
the odyssey is the river, it's sad but true
love is lust and lust is love
flowing free with Kristen Blue
I guess I should have realized
beauty leaves me hypnotized
yellow are the distant fragile memories
that make the future long overdue

Red is the color that I think of
when I think of blue
when I think of you
because red is the color of loneliness
it is true, my lovely Kristen Blue
and when you are old and lonely
you'll realize that the flower never grew
because you were so afraid to let
anybody deep inside of you
With all the wealth, all the freedom
will anybody be there
for the lovely Kristen Blue
She may not believe but I know that it's true
in this world there is only us;
and the lovely Kristen Blue

She blew me away like a dandelion
in a hot summer dream
with her elegant moistened lips

Breakout

Do you know what you're doing to me?
Turning visions into reality
She may not be my soul
less toxic than love
but somehow, I feel as though
I am one (undone) or two (through)
when I am with the lovely Kristen Blue

Please don't where any clothes
for nakedness is a rose
held in your hand with a smile
oh, I'll
do anything it is true
for the lovely Kristen Blue
How many times must I fake this love
before you'll take this love
deep inside of you
my lovely Kristen Blue

Hue
Subdue
Pursue
Cue (if she picks it up)
Misconstrue
Flew
(the cards she) Drew
Please take my heart and break it in two
if that's what you're good at,
that's what you should do
and when you come to my funeral
take off your black laced lingerie
and throw it on in my grave
for 'tis everything I've ever wanted
but could never have.

Victor V. Valenote

# Laughing at Your Denial

Billions of worlds within a billion trillion stars;
billions of people, each with their own disguise.
How is it that we've come to meet?
How is it that I've seen your eyes?
I'd like to sit by a river, tell you stories,
and laugh at your denial.
I'd like to pierce the veil
running naked, running wild
in some far-off corner of a dream
of moral turpitude.
In my icy formal solitude
there is a message I'd like to send.
Save me girl, save me girl
from the fabled futile end.
Being here with you
is like sniffing rubber glue
early in the morning.
Some are born to suffer pain;
some are born to drink the rain
early in the morning.
But of all the people I've ever met
you're the one I'll never forget;
walls are forming.
Such is the mystery of initiation,
such is the strangeness of perturbation.
Perhaps it has already been said to you,
that in the end the love you will forsake
is certain to be greater than the love you take.
She has shown me the reality;
life comes with no guarantee.
The greatest woman in the world
is a kind-hearted woman.
She will never let you down.

# The Last Ride

to not respect the passion
of a human/human hunt
is to not respect humanity
is to not respect yourself
we are all on a/the hunt

he had been looking at her closely
he smiled and she smiled
but only her smile was real
it was a hazy afternoon
and the snake lurked in the bushes
his head peering through two blades of grass

he watched
as she agreed to take a ride
and blow a kiss to the snake
as she rode out of sight
into the heat of the horizon
to the back of night

Victor V. Valenote

# If Only Just Good-bye

He thought her a queen,
she thought him just plain;
so, he went home lonely
and cried in the rain.
Yet, what makes love flower
but tears of pain.

So, he gave her roses
as in a medieval play;
he did not say who it was
with feelings this way.
He was afraid she'd be disappointed
and throw his heart away.

His passion he must hide,
in her presence he must pretend;
because he thinks that if he tells her
of what he does intend
she would feel as though
the world was coming to an end.

But he thinks about her all day,
how life is cruel and unfair;
he thinks about her all night,
fingers running through his hair.
he wonders what she thinks of,
if she is completely unaware.

He offers her his innocence,
there is no need to ask him why;
amongst her delicate beauty,
he sits, silent and shy;
waiting and waiting to hear her voice
if only just good-bye.

# The Ghost of a Lost Love's Soul c. 1740, London, coming to greet an unknown suicide victim

Run with a ceremonious gallop
across green grass......
with little yellow flowers
trample upon my loves soul
like a ghost horse in the skies
sun rise, some rise
despite the pain of memories
like a sharp blade
through the eyes
like icicles
melting inside your head
melting......melting......
and when they're gone, they're gone.
When it all washes away......you're dead
from the pain of a love
that has been lost
my body tossed
into another hole
to be covered some day
with green grass......
and little yellow flowers.

Victor V. Valenote

# Beyond Survival (not another waterfall)

Floating down a river of love
heading straight for a waterfall
the current is too strong for me
I cannot move, I cannot see......at all.

when I reach the edge
I'll think of you,
think of the things we use to do
it seems so insane
how you gave me so much rain
when all I asked for was a drink.

I'm sink, sink, sinking fast
I should've known it couldn't last
and now the visions of the past
are waiting out in front of me.
'Tis all the same;
the black prisms and the poetry.
I wish you could've read between the lines;
the twisted, tortured, growing vines.
You never gave an effort, you never tried
perhaps, perhaps that is why we died.
You never seemed to realize
the monkey passion in disguise.
True feeling is hidden in the eyes,
the eyes of the crescent moon.

To everyone out in front,
and to everyone left behind;
I understand your situation
but would you mind
throwing me a rope or just wave good-bye.
I am not sure exactly why
or what it would actually take
to turn this river into a lake
But please do it soon

Breakout

before the horizon meets the moon
because I'm floating down this river of love
heading straight for another waterfall
the current is too strong for me
I cannot move, I cannot see......at all.
Yet this time, babe
I'm going to a lake of serenity
this time, babe
I'm taking you with me.

# To the Wolves

The wisdom for today......
take your fears away,
and breed them in the pasture with your sorrow.
The wisdom of tomorrow......
take their children to the fire,
and let them play with your desire.

Moreover, the common soul is saddened by another day
gone without an accomplishment......and why?
Why should the individual care?
Why should the group care?
For what is an accomplishment......
discovering a cure for misery,
having an orgasm,
losing a few pounds,
winning the lottery,
reading a classic novel,
putting a cigar out in the face of your dreams,
writing another mediocre poem like this?
What is it to whomever......and why?

And so it goes......the very next
person closest to death
figured it all out.
He got back into bed and tried to sleep.
If he were only able to handle the responsibility......
and somewhere in the midst of that thought
an orgasm occurs
and soon after......another.
Very possibly, a necessary one.

And somewhere......a child
lies angry, kicking, and screaming.

And somewhere......a child
lies in quiet comfort.

And somewhere......a child lies
listless and disheartened.

And somewhere......a mother-to-be
sits happy with her husband at her side.

And somewhere......a mother-to-be
wonders if her husband will find out the child is not his.

And somewhere......a mother-to-be
doesn't know who the father is.

And somewhere...... a mother-to-be
is thrown from a tumbling car.

And somewhere......a woman weeps
that she cannot bear a child.

And somewhere......a father
prays for a son.

And somewhere......a father
throws himself to the wolves.

Victor V. Valenote

# Throw Caution to the Wind

I met an old man in the park.

Do you believe in love at first sight?

I said,
I know when I see a curve,
the soft delicate curve of the back......
of her eyes.

Why don't you give her your heart?

Well, for one thing,
you know I haven't a heart.

On the contrary sir......
I know that your heart is broken,
but any of your parts and pieces
would be more than she's ever had.

# April May

she brings me beautiful
rain-flower(ing) smiles
her cheek so soft
the burning daylight creeps
though my window
to define its perfection
resting on my shoulder
her hair
a world within
running fingers through
a dream

Victor V. Valenote

# Mutiny on Floor Twenty-Nine

Mutiny on the sinking ship.
I am not here to punish the disorder,
Mr. Death in the captain's quarter.

Do you let the children survive?
It is not their time to arrive,
but they will go on without you.

If I touch you like
you've never been touched before,
would you roll with me......
out the door of perception?
The door that surrounds you.
The door that confounds you.

A brain-dead cat on floor twenty-nine
staring out of a window.
It sure looks fine all around you.

Feel the swirl on her inner thighs
and you'll see how love never dies
around you, all around you.

You can tip your hat to experience,
but how are you going to get
over this barbed wire fence?
It's all around you, look all around you.

Put your money on black or red,
and as sure as the sun burns
you'll wind up dead.
Then, just maybe then,
your poetry will be read
by the few remaining survivors.

# Plastic Songs in the Broken Ceremony

It was lasting and long and it wasn't too quiet
tell-tale dreams and you cannot deny it
an ancient breeze, a mystic glow
incandescent spew and lava flow
what else does she know
about you.

recording glimpses of a tiring life
murder is reason, who invented the knife
He stifled the jury with infinite wisdom
it pays to have the forgotten kingdom
all around you.

Call me desperate and void
naked heartache, gone, destroyed.
We do not realize the significance
of the red, red dawn.
Until we have nothing left
everything is gone.
without you.
Gone without you

Victor V. Valenote

# Where are you, Sister Blue

Into my eyes......
back inside you're going to crawl.
Look out, heaven's going to fall.
Spread your legs, everywhere there is snow;
hold your hands out, it is going slow.
She runs for cover, she runs right under
everything she wanted to be.
You're running wild, you silly child,
telling stories of ramparts in the sky.
You are caught in the crosshairs
of a dream, a silly scheme
trying to rectify your life.

I see a bloody white cat,
a lion on the side of the road.
Blood stained highway,
everywhere I sing your ode;
take my life at the next crossing.
White cat in disguise,
deathly peering.
Every time I try to get away
you are right there by my side.

# Forgetfulness

Forgive and forget,
you do not need;
forget to forgive,
the latest creed.

Forgetfulness thrives
when nothing will matter;
silver and cold,
the teeth that chatter.

No pain is present
when all forgotten;
no outlandish outburst
when teeth get rotten.

Forgive with all your heart
if you choose never to forget,
the pain will pulsate through your jaw
as clenching consumes regret.

Victor V. Valenote

# Red, Red, Dawn

Now you come to me
but do you know how I feel;
now you come to me
but there's nothing left to steal.
I remember how you told me
how much you wanted to be free,
but you couldn't right now
you just couldn't......right now.
And now, now is long gone;
so, I wrote down this song
for you......you to come to me.
Although you know how I feel,
please come to me
though there's nothing left to steal.
Would you promise me,
would you promise me?
When I wake up......red, red, dawn;
when I wake up and your gone,
would you promise me?
Would you promise me
that you'll just leave a letter?
It would make me feel much better
to know you couldn't look me in the eye,
and say the last goodbye.
I know you understand
the simple phrase, 'a bird in the hand',
but you know what I say?
I'll take the two in the bush any old day
if the one in the hand is a dove,
because I'm sick and tired of love.
The notion just tears me apart;
the hurt it takes to start......
start it all over again......
start it all over again.

# Wobble-wobble-wobble......Flip

She thinks of you as a child.

Wobble-wobble-wobble......
Flip!

She thinks that the heart
is just a toy......
that you wind-up,
and give to somebody
to play with for a while......

Wobble-wobble-wobble......
Flip!

Wobble-wobble-wobble......
Flip!

......until you seemingly get bored,
and toss it into the blue bin
in the back of your closet.

Or perhaps......
while lying around unnoticed
for quite some time,
the dog gets a hold of it
and tears it to bits.

Victor V. Valenote

# The Erotic Nightmare

......and so, the erotic nightmare sinks in;
to the back of the neck, a casual hook.
The pain, excruciating, comes with each heartbeat;
exceeding expectation, you come for a closer look.
Weakened and wilting, my body is willing;
For one lasting moment, for lost days of leisure;
But my mind, my soul, my good ol'......will;
......lying still......lying still, waiting for pleasure.

A wild pack of dogs tearing at my legs;
someday for something, everyone begs.
Everyone is prey and everyone must bleed;
upon something, we all need to feed.
I guess I've never seen so much blood;
the pool of dreams that I now lie in.
Floating and floating, floating and floating;
the pool of dreams, I now may die in.

Using every remnant of hopeless sanity;
I'll explain the situation with minimal profanity.
But we can all have a lapse, inevitable perhaps;
such is the fate of each waning breath.
So, my eyes burn, burn from a red liquid
that is just as symbolic of life, as it is of death.

Hands everywhere, slowly pull me down;
Letting me live, but hoping I'll drown.
Prodding and groping, fondling and stroking;
Blood in my lungs, I feel like I'm choking.

The ancient wonder, pulling me under;
pleasure striking like a bolt of lightning.
And between the pleasure, a dose of pains;
between the thunder, the pouring rains
......the clutching reigns of love.

# Breakout

Not a soul around, not even a trace;
I lift my head to see a pretty face.
The hook sinks in deeper, 'tis a beauty decapitated;
the back of her skull visually dilapidated.
Her tongue keeping me erect through all the pain;
with thunder and lighting, and pouring rain.

With each crack of lightning a jerk and explosion;
the never lasting joy, followed by erosion.
My body jerks, explodes, explodes, and explodes;
and erodes, and erodes, and erodes, and erodes.
The demon just glares, and stares ever smiling;
the smile of Mona Lisa, intriguing......beguiling.

Tadpole-size sperm, streaming......a fountain;
all over everything, background......a mountain.
Up and down my body, she uses her tongue in kind;
I feel torn flesh from her neck, right behind.

Working her way to my face......Princess Reaper;
I try to turn but the hooks sink deeper.
Forcing her tongue in my mouth to my demise;
I want to close my eyes......but I don't.
Kissing the demon, ruggedly mouthed;
The nightmare continues, again, I am aroused.

A torso is lowered down by chains;
old and wet, and rotting remains.
Onto my erection, no choice but willing;
up and down, with sounds so chilling.
Two demons, one on each side;
working chains on a pulley, to the beat of drums.
One pulls and the torso moves up;
the other pulls and back down, it comes.

Up and down, up and down, countless, immeasurable;
Up and down, up and down, until it is pleasurable.
I can feel another orgasm coming, in relentless hell;
this time piercing, striking an artesian well.

Victor V. Valenote

The demons disappear, and the body collapses;
and I come, and I come, and I come......time elapses.

It must be hours now of continual orgasm;
Spasm after spasm, into eternal phantasm.
I come and I come until the explosion, cyclone;
blood and flesh everywhere, and a little bit of bone.

I lift my head just a bit, to see my erection;
Still spewing blood with forceful ejection.
Never stopping, it keeps going, and going, and going;
Floating higher in the room, blood ever-flowing.
Only a few more inches, up to my chin;
over my head, the concrete ceiling closing in.
......and such is the erotic nightmare.

# The Small of Your Back

The last time I asked
who you were,
......I noticed
the lonely kiss,
as my hand went down
the small of your back.

Over elegant curves,
over glistening eyes,
we are all responsible
for our own demise.

Curves of love
in the back of your mind,
......the bind-ing
together of two lost souls.

Victor V. Valenote

# Imagine a Dream (a song for April)

Imagine a girl
while lying on your back
with your head in the clouds.
Imagine a man
who always understands
just how you feel.
Imagine a touch
so gentle and so pure
it sends a chill up your spine.
Imagine a song
of love, and of passion
written especially for you.
Imagine a girl
so beautiful, so perfect,
but never having truly been loved.
Imagine a road
that goes on forever, and ever, and ever,
leading to the depths of darkened eyes.
Imagine a smile
that glows in light, and could spite the world
in the beat of a heart grown cold.
Imagine a land
filled with rivers and givers, and slivers
of sunshine flowers everywhere.
Imagine a man
who comes in from the dark,
and steals your heart away, so far away.
Imagine a soul
so sincere and so true you cannot believe
it is you, that he wants to be free.

# Burying Alive

I need thirty-four
more poems
to reach my goal.
Fill up the hole,
the incessant hole
......in my head.
Just when I think
I am nearing the end,
patting the top down
with my shovel;
just when I think
......I buried the dead,
more and more air.
Dread, oh dread
the hole in my head,
true and tried, opens wide.
A hand reaches up,
grabs my ankle,
and thirty-four more
turns to thirty-five.
Another failed attempt
At burying alive.

# The Gambler

Oh, what am I doing
hanging on the window ledge?
I never knew a morning that
couldn't offer up some thrills.
The lake is rumbling,
I think it's going to blow.
The maid is humming
she takes two hundred-dollar bills.

The situation dissolves
like honey in my tea.
The storm clouds are coming,
I watch you disappear.
The ocean is a mirror,
I see my eyeballs floating in the sky.
And you keep on running
because you live a life of fear.

The chain gang shuffles on
singing a song about hope and fate.
One killed the other,
and ended up here with me.
If you step on a rattlesnake
don't complain about the bite.
Nature does what it has to do,
put an end to the misery.

The train rolls by
the same time every day.
The waterman planned his escape
before he ever arrived.
The lonely ladies live to love,
and he always left to live.
Life, a roll, and a bottle......
add freedom, they seem contrived.

Journeys always come to an end
whenever you want them to.
Opportunity presents itself
in the most simplistic way.
He burns his rags and riches
in an old wood stove.
All for the early morning rain,
and the softest bet of the day.

Victor V. Valenote

# Spellbound

I know a graveyard woman
she keeps a jar by her bed.
A jar filled with fingers and toes;
bits and pieces of the dead.
She never cracks a smile,
but her lips are always rosy red.

If I ask her to love me
she says, you know I always will.
Remember why I come here,
lying motionless and still.
Tell me ancient high hero,
who's next on your list to kill?

Sunday morning in the Quarter,
voodoo whispers in the hall.
From the third-floor window,
he hears a beckoning call.
Black iron fencing and spikes,
the unlucky piercing fall.

# The Undefeated One

I can see the faded lines
underneath her eyes,
hard loving is the worst disguise.
Someday you'll wake up
and realize,
love slowly bleeds out
until it dies.
In the heat of the moment
she could never say no,
and youth passed on by
with nothing to show.
One night and one night soon,
Venus and Mars
dance with the moon.

It's been a mighty smooth ride
for the ungrateful old man,
sailing through life on a catamaran.
But, Father Time grumbles
underneath his breath,
a forty-foot wave
and an instant death.
Looking at the sky,
learning your fear;
what appeared far away
now seems near.
The fool travels on
with a smile on his face;
never knowing first or last,
or about the race.

Victor V. Valenote

# Summer Fling

Much of hatred
Much of the day after
Much of why I left you
lying there
The heated moment found you
Overflowing with effervescence
Filled with all I have to give
And to give
is all I need to live
But to live I know
that you need something more
Something to hold and cling
But such is
A summer fling

# Office Life

Back from a four-day weekend
Back to the shit
The big shit
The biggest shit smell of all
Back to getting up at the ass crack of dawn
Driving in the herd like cattle
Back to the stupid building
Back to the black chair
The computer screens
The stupid fucking mouse
Stupid fucking emails
The stupid fucking phone messages
And the stupidest fucking meetings
Back to middle school politics
Back to the shit
The shit of an office life

Victor V. Valenote

# The Oak Tree

I like the way
you use your fingertips
I like the way
you lick your lips
I like the way
your eyes fall upon my soul
For whom that bell did toll
Woke up like a stuck pig
Sweating
In the midst of night
Letting
A poem
Jettison from my head
To my phone
Awkward instant
In an old home
A little beer
Erases the fear
Fear of fear and regret
A little more beer
I am not afraid of regret

When I'm not inside of you
I don't know what to do
The world spins endlessly
Slowly grows the oak tree
In the back yard of my mind
Keep searching
Keep searching
What can you find
Regret puts your head in a sling
Regret is easy to see
Regret
Hanging from the tree

# A Good Morning from Hell

I woke up with a pain in my side
The left side, the right side
Stumbled down to make some coffee
My head hurts, my eyes are bloody
While brewing I turned to empty the dishwasher

The largest most endless dishwasher
Ever known
Rack after rack
As deep as the darkness
would let me see
Climbing in, flashlight in hand
Sorting through buckets
Of silverware and plasticware
Curled up and melted
All over the floor

My coffee overflowing on the counter

Plate after plate
Bowl after bowl
Opening drawer after drawer
Door after door
Searching endlessly for
The proper resting place
Of each item

My coffee overflowing on the counter

The dim light of dawn
The dim light of dusk
Glows through the cracks in the wall
Day after day
Week after week

My coffee overflowing on the counter

# The Celibate Man

Let me go
Let me die
Tonight, right now
Let me see
Let me know
what I've always known
That hell is an upgrade

Beneath the fire
And melting jade
Satan's daughter
Waiting to get laid

Though Heaven is better
Better than hell
Hell is better than here
All the same but getting laid
Once a week
Or once a year
Ever again
If what I see can be mine for a moment
Then give me hell
The last serenade
Even with the hooks and chains
Hell is an upgrade

# Lost Memory Gained

I once met you
Inside of a sugar cube
With hand and lube
And heart constrained
Emerald lost memory gained
My whole life grew
Inside a torn and giant shoe
Across the sky persistence flew
Not expecting a thing
Up and down I watched your ring
Yellow shiny and bright
Supernova in the night......sky
I never asked you why
I never asked you why
Insanity......I never knew how much
Insanity......you left me out of touch
With insanity
You are my broken crutch
Leaning on the window sill

Victor V. Valenote

# Inside

Everywhere rain falls in silence
Silently our troubles rescind
Expectations lost in the asylum
Beckoning the autumn wind

The autumn wind is here
I don't give a damn
I don't know where I'm going
And you don't know where I am

# Royal Companion

Fuck the royal fuck of it all
Fuck all my typewriters
Fuck them all
Looking at me
Like the most tempting sirens
in all the world
You see this
You see this
You just keep looking

At that which you cannot attain

Hell
This is a living hell
The only thing that could make it so

I know where I am

The man in the mirror
Picks up a razor and smiles
The image goes on
For miles and miles
The hand on my head
Turns all the dials

A big red mess
Left on the tiles

Victor V. Valenote

# Before You're Old

When the blue sky
Gets through with me
And when the snow transpires
The black and white fires
Fill the room
Lasting forever in my head
Is the blurred vision
Parting me
Good and bad......division

In a daze the cold, cold mirror
Screams
Yeaaaah
I need you......your soul sold
I want you......tell-tale told
I'll kill you......before you're old
Yeaaaah

When the rain filters through
The dark dusty earth
The mirth down below
Ceremony for the few
Ceremony just for you
What my will has become
Whatever it takes to
Keep you from
I see me, I see you
I see one, I see two

In a daze the cold, cold mirror
Screams
Yeaaaah
I need you......your soul sold
I want you......tell-tale told
I'll kill you......before you're old
Yeaaaah

And you try, try to run
Turn around, see the setting sun
Chasing you
Chasing you
Chasing you
You can't hide, you can't hide
The darkness from inside
Follow through
Follow through
The moment comes to you
See the soul in the empty glass
See your whole life slowly pass

In a daze the cold, cold mirror
Screams
Yeaaaah
I need you......your soul sold
I want you......tell-tale told
I'll kill you......before you're old
Yeaaaah

Victor V. Valenote

# On and On it Goes

Take my sunny so, so day
Throw it face down on the way
I wish......I could go
Back in time before I met you
I......would never let you
Fall for me.

I......would never wonder
Of the distant blunder
The river drags me under
Flowing free.

# The Monkey-Faced Spider

And now you know why you're here
Not to live in pain and fear
Set the controls to crazy land
My hand
My hand
shakes uncontrollably
The greatest mystery
Solved
Dissolved under the tongue
Behind closed doors
And eyes
An island
Sinking slowly until
It disappears
The daylight disappears
I know the evening
Sings in silence
Brings its oceans
Overhead
The dying time is dead
The monkey-faced spider
In my head reigns, supreme
Crawling
      Climbing
Crawling
      Climbing
Crawling
      Climbing

Victor V. Valenote

# Hippopotomonstrosesquipedaliophobia

She is so kind
one who can see
much like me
Sun, you
Old soul
Saw in two
The turn key
To my soul
My id
My ego
My urn

See it
Get out of my way
Shy eyes
Let me put my day
In you
Over you
Let me in
Let my mad ink
Use you

This odd day
New, now
Has me
Lost
But for her lie
All can own her
But few
Can get to her

She is how
I say, 'live!'
She is how I
Stay me
If one day is bad

Breakout

So, can I die
So, can she cry
And let me see why

Shot of rye
Shot of rye
We met at the pub
Had ham on rye
Shot of rye
Shot of rye
Back to her pad
In the tub
In the bed
It can be said
The one who will die
Will win.

Victor V. Valenote

# Another Wad of Paper

Shika clack
Shika shika clack
What a giant sack
of shit
What a giant sack
of it
The sack of life
I lug around
over my shoulder
dragging on the ground
slowly behind

This wad of paper
crumpled as it is
in part
in whole
in sole possession,
and forever unique
Degrading, as you allow
Lasting, as you allow
Seen, as you allow

Cc: yourself

# On the Sea Floor

Here is a heart
In a seashell
Thumping
Here is a heart
Consistently pumping
Waiting for the
Inevitable confrontation
With the soul sucking squid
Worming
Squirming
In search of scum
At the bottom of the earth

The heart looks
Delicately tempting and tasty
Yet
Ticking snickering
Desperately insistent and
Ready for blood
Closely guarding
Love in the mud

The battle short-lived
As predicted
The poison befouls
And so
Dead on the sea floor
The squid slowly rots
The heart leans back
And lets out a roar
Calling all victims
Who know not what's in-store
When they find the seashell
On the sea floor

Victor V. Valenote

# Never Before the Sacrifice

Everybody new
The memory filled with glue
No more than a week
Tweak the truth and then
Rebirth of a message
To send
Everyone pretend
The means to the end
Walking around
Needles and pins
Floating on hopeless grins
I wish I knew
The girl from Lake Havasu
Remember what to do
When stranded in broken time
Between distance
And darkness sublime
Luckily there are few
Like me and you
Drunk on fire and ice
Do it once
Do it twice

Never before the sacrifice

# Exhale

Man will never forget his wounds
Time will continue to breathe
Long after he waves goodbye
Time stops for no one
Time stops for no thing
Time stops for no reason
The grave consequence
Of a single human's
Perception of time
In his own lifetime
What of 500 years from now
Irrelevant fiction
What of 500 billion years from now
Oh, Humanity
We are but spermatozoa
Seeking out an egg
In the understanding of time
I heard the physicist
Lecture of global climate change
I stared out of the window
Watching a sparrow build a nest
Knowing that sparrow
Would not exist in a few years
The sun glaring down on me
Knowing it will not exist
In a few billion years
I hear only the echo in my mind
The sound of a ticking clock
The sound that never happened
I hear my heart thumping in harmony
Laughing at the narcissism
Of my own humanity

Victor V. Valenote

# The Land of Dick and Jane

I need something else
to make the pain go away
I need something new
something sane
Widespread felicity
beholding my sanctity
By the grace of god
unfolding with the need
Somewhere to leave
the seed
Floating on an on
tomorrow never knows
What to become
without being pushed around
Give me one more hour to perform
reborn in another universe
The first universe
for all to see
Someday you will understand
what it was
Someday you will understand
that it was not me
Lurking about
in this strange land

# Sail on, Silver Smile

Every now and again
I go back to Stoney Isle
Visions of yesterday
waiting with a portrait of your smile
But yesterday sold a bill of goods
took off with the future's wife
Left the butcher reaching behind
to pull out his favorite knife
And me, I'm still sailing on
Sail on distant sea
No one knows who I am
Or where I want to be

Victor V. Valenote

# On My Way Home

Sitting here beating on broken promises
Drums made of thickened skin from me
I waited for you on tomorrow's death bed
I waited for you on wounded knee
Looking to the future ever uncertain
Oh, where are you tonight......my misery

Anybody could be like you, shining princess
Walking all over my eyes exuberantly
But the sky floats on endless empty heartaches
While your dark somber mends my sanity
Every picture reminds me of misfortune
Oh, where are you tonight......my misery

The undertaker reads your red love line
Sunshine runs the other way to be free
There's something about the silence in your nightmare
Turns your soulless guise toward me
The rain man never gives up his devotion
Oh, where are you tonight......my misery

Your black hair and black eyes make me crazy
Sometimes my life skips a beat in harmony
The freight train goes through the Melancholy Mountains
Skulls and bones scattered as far as I can see
I don't care if I ever make it out of here
On my way home to you......my misery

# Taking Precedence

I see a blonde and a brunette
Either one would be fine for me
Tonight
Average loveliness
Average looks at best
Desperation always lowers
Our expectation

Which one
You'll have to guess
But one doesn't mind
The other does
Take advantage of what is
And make it what was
So, in the darkness of the evening
Rustling in my bed
My lustful need takes precedence
And again, is slowly fed

Victor V. Valenote

# Halfway to My Sundown

If I had a truck for all my dreams
I would pack it until busting at the seams
Overflowing heading down the road
I'd dump them off at the local landfill

Then I would drive across the Americas
Pick up all the broken pieces of all the dreams
Littered in every ditch and along every stream
Fill up every landfill in every town

Drop off each knew one as it comes
If I had a truck for all my dreams
I wouldn't have that much to show
No
I wouldn't have that much to show

# Perhaps You

Oh, the mankind
Humankind
He she it kind
The person
The animal
We all are
With teeth
Canines longing
To sink into
Someone
Something
Perhaps you

Victor V. Valenote

# The First Five Seconds

Five seconds before
my heart stops
I'll think of the
mass of nothing
that ended before me
Five seconds too soon

Five days before
my eyeballs feed worms
I'll remember the
last time I smiled
a bit of reality

Sadly though,
five easy pieces
plays out
in a slow momentum of
Five-minute bursts

Five minutes on
Five minutes off

Five minutes on
Five minutes off

Five days later
I have no eyes
I fall in love again
and I look around
for a reason to believe
in the first five seconds

# A Ten-Minute Poem

Left on the dashboard
of my brain
Frying in the summer sun
No one
can see it
For what it is worth
No one
hears its beckoning
No one
feels its desperation
No one
takes the time
No one bothers
to presume

Go on
make some room inside
Go for another ride
Move it over
to the passenger's side
for a while
Then toss it out of the window
with a cigarette butt

A few sparks of light
A flicker......
and then it is gone

Set in its proper place
to begin the process of decay

Victor V. Valenote

# I Wonder If God Has a Patent

What do you think happens when you die?
Nothing?
Nothing is nothingness
and completely misunderstood
Nothing is a concept differs
Mine, yours, or someone else's?
Heaven, hell, or purgatory?
Mine, yours, or someone else's?
Out of the concept Absolute Nothingness
comes the invention of gods, religions, and belief systems

Off to the underworld of eternal life with the darkened gods
Directly to Hades to become shade in the Isles of Blest
Becoming re-dead with no hope of resurrection

Reincarnation......into what?
What you want, what someone else wants, or pure randomness?
Release from a cycle of rebirth
to attain union with the ultimate reality

Maybe nothing really dies
and you just convince yourself that you are dead

Perhaps a toy drinking bird
forever pecks your soul
But this time the design is
in perpetual motion

# Another stupid fucking poem that starts with 'and'

And the anger within
Makes us gentle again
Trying to live the quiet sin
Knowing how to lose
Love mixed with gin
Remember the truth
And consequence
It takes a society
to learn to pillage
It takes an idiot
To teach a village

Victor V. Valenote

# Misanthropic Optics

Belief systems are like assholes
Everybody needs one
and they all excrete shit
When combined with overpopulation
the shit must be disposed of properly
or it become a detriment to the larger group at hand
Thus, the enemy of the belief system
lies in the dichotomy of space and time
decaying and rotting

Capitalism is an incurable disease running rampant
the scourge of humanity......zombie folklore
individually ending, only when the brain ceases to fire
Socialism is its evil twin
Bicker and squabble
Squabble squabble squabble
Individualism vs. collectivism

'Ologies and isms'
are just like assholes
Everybody has got one
and everyone's is better
than everyone else's

So, be careful where you
point your crooked finger
You know how many people there are
Of small and midsize businesses
In the service sector
Riding on the 'Corporatania Nervosa'
Serving assholes nonetheless
How many greedy lying cheating
Pig fucking scumbags
Cum-filled condoms
with front-row reservations to
the lowest rungs of hell

96

Breakout

Many to most
cheating on their spouses
cheating on taxes
Treating their family like
a pile of piss-ants
Don't even know their kids
Living for selling
a worthless pathetic
service of some sort
What a great gift to humanity
How would the world
survive without them

Be careful where you
point your crooked finger
I'll break it off and shove it
up your fucking ass
but you might like it
So, I will use a broomstick instead
After all, in the whole
scheme of things
you really are only as important
as a broomstick
with a head of lettuce
stuck on top
So, be careful where you
point your crooked finger

Victor V. Valenote

# Uncovering the Future

The Digger
The Mountain
Or
I am the Excavator
Operator of
the massive Bucyrus RH400

Put all the zealot politicals
in a stadium and let them fight
barehanded to death

Scoop them out
when they are dead
and send more in
until every last one
has killed each other

Keep piling them up
outside the arena

Cover them with dirt
making a mountain
as high as any other

# Self-Recognition

writing is a disease
that slowly sinks in
through the brain
fueled by the common thread
of human pain
a pain that changes a man
a pain that changes a sub-culture
a pain that changes the soul of a society
sometimes the pain is self-recognized
sometimes it is not
and when it is
you get greatness

# So Many Things

The fact that you are
so many things......
the only thing
I don't know how to get;
the only thing I would like to have;
the only thing I have no idea
what to say to.
The only thing that I can be used by
for a while,
while I go back and forth
between the lines
of a sudden urge to leave......
and the other side
of the best way to live.
Many words can be used
to describe you......
except true
Many have lied and died for you;
as many have denied your value.

# Get Up and Go

Every night
while I lie in bed
Eyes closed
but wide awake
In my head
writing poem after poem
I realize that......
the new version
of night time
is much better than
the lighter side of the day
My alarm goes off
and I must
get up and go
Off to work
For what purpose......
to do the same thing
over and over
again, and again
for the rest of my known life

# The Last Prayer

Oh God
God of fuck
God of art
Give me a moment
One last moment
One more moment
To perform in the
Arena of content
Let me in
Let me in
Into the void
Let me create
The only thing I know
The thing that lasts eternal
Let me battle the mortality
Of artistic endeavor
Let me fill the void
One more time
Let me die
In peaceful coexistence
With a naked canvas
At my side

# About the Author

Born and raised in a residue of malcontent, Victor V. Valenote left a promising life of mediocrity for the adventures of pursuing a similar fate in the vast expanse of the Great North. He has been living in Eagle River, Alaska ever since, and is forever afflicted with the rare, incurable disease so commonly known as......poetry.

**Thomas Walker Publications**
Eagle River, Alaska

www.ingramcontent.com/pod-product-compliance
Lightning Source LLC
Chambersburg PA
CBHW070639030426
42337CB00020B/4079